ONE DIRECTION

Midnight Memories

MARY BOONE

TRIUMPH
BOOKS

This book is available in quantity at special discounts for your group or organization. For further information, contact:

Triumph Books LLC
814 North Franklin Street
Chicago, Illinois 60610
Phone: (312) 337-0747
www.triumphbooks.com

Printed in U.S.A.

ISBN: 978-1-62937-019-4

Content developed and packaged by Rockett Media, Inc.
Writer: Mary Boone
Editor: Bob Baker
Design: Andrew Burwell
Cover design by Andrew Burwell

Photographs courtesy of AP Images
unless otherwise noted

ONE DIRECTION

Midnight Memories

CHAPTER ONE
FIVE BECOME ONE

The cheeky son of an Irish butcher. The dark and handsome lad from Bradford, England. The Wolverhampton boy who wouldn't let health challenges keep him from becoming a confident performer. The chap who was known for singing in the corridors of his Holmes Chapel high school. The prankster who got suspended from classes for exposing his bare bum during a theater production.

Who could have imagined these five very different guys would come together to become One Direction? Who wants to imagine how different today's music scene would be if they hadn't?

By now, you know their story: These five strangers – Niall Horan, Zayn Malik, Liam Payne, Harry Styles and Louis Tomlinson – individually auditioned for 2010's *The X Factor*. They made it through the show's preliminary competitions but were cut at the boot camp stage. And that's when the judges threw them a lifeline of sorts; they could continue to compete as a group. The boys all agreed to give it a try and the rest, as they say, is history.

No, they didn't win that season of *The X Factor*, but they've undoubtedly become the show's most famous third-place finishers. In the four years since meeting on that televised talent show, the guys of One Direction have released three albums – and all three have debuted at No. 1. Even more astonishing: By the end of 2014, the

numbers-crunchers at *Business Insider* predict One Direction will be the first boy band in history to earn more than $1 billion in a year through the sale of CDs, DVDs, concert tickets, movie tickets and merchandise.

Who are these billion-dollar men? We're so glad you asked:

Niall Horan

Niall James Horan was born September 13, 1993, in Mullingar in County Westmeath, located in the north-central part of Ireland. His parents divorced when he was just five. His father worked – and still does – as a butcher. His mother worked at Mullingar Pewter and has since remarried.

Even as a young boy, Niall had star quality.

Niall's cousin, Robert Horan, told the (London) *Daily Mail* in 2010 that he'd always thought Niall would end up in show business.

quick-witted, always yapping away."

When Niall decided to try his luck at *The X Factor* auditions, it was with the full support of his family, friends and teachers. His grandmother and mother escorted

"Even when he was a young child, I said to myself, 'That lad is going to end up on the stage' – though I always thought he'd end up being a comedian," Robert said. "Niall was always really outgoing and

him to Dublin, where he tried out with his rendition of "So Sick of Love Songs" and his close-knit family was in the audience to support him throughout all stages of the competition.

Much has changed in the four years

since Niall first stepped onto *The X Factor* stage. Yet, much has remained the same.

Anonymity is long gone. These days, thousands of fans – many of them adoring young women – show up wherever Niall goes: the beach, the mall, a pub. He's also grown used to tabloid articles chronicling his romances – or alleged romances – with singer Demi Lovato, singer/actress Selena Gomez, songstress Ellie Goulding, Hungarian model Barbara Palvin, TV presenter Amanda Byram and Harry Style's ex-girl-friend, Alahna Alridge.

All that media scrutiny might send some folks into seclusion. But Niall still loves to do "normal things."

"I like to go to gigs and concerts and stuff. Just hanging out with friends and jamming on the guitar," he told *Kidzworld* in August 2013. "I've recently started teaching myself how to play the drums so I have a drum kit now in my house and I wake up the neighbors and they're not very happy (about it)."

That high-energy boy who once entertained his family is now a high-energy lad who entertains the world.

Says writer/producer Savan Kotecha: "He just bounces off the walls and has not changed one bit – he'll always be Niall."

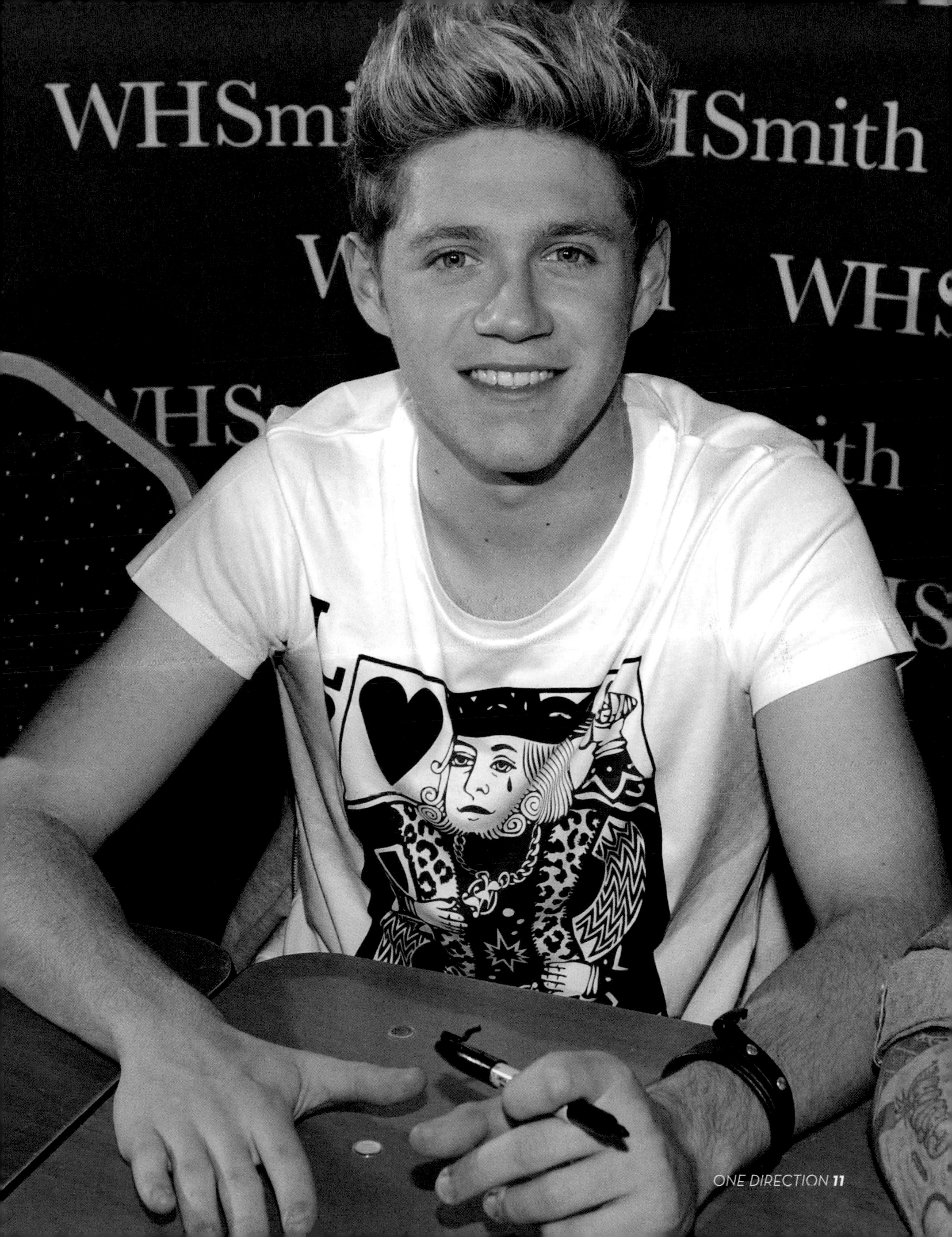

ONLY ONE DIRECTION

Matt Brinkler, Henry Allan, Jamie Searls, Aaron Foster and David Ribi are selling out concert halls and thrilling fans with renditions of songs like "Up All Night" and "Best Song Ever." These guys aren't One Direction, but they're getting paid to impersonate 1D.

Only One Direction is a tribute band; hundreds of young men auditioned to be part of the group when it was assembled two years ago. The guys have learned every song the boy band has released and perform one-hour sets jammed with 1D's biggest hits.

Just like the real One Direction, Only One Direction members are met at gigs by thousands of screaming female fans.

"They storm the stage afterwards wanting pictures and autographs. It's crazy," Matt Brinkler, who performs as Louis Tomlinson, told the (London) *Daily Mail* in February 2014.

Aaron Foster who performs as Liam Payne, added: "The reaction of people when we perform is crazy. It's mental - when there are girls crying, they want you to touch their hands and sign their skin – it's a really surreal experience."

Zayn Malik

Born January 12, 1993, in Bradford, West Yorkshire, England, Zayn Jawaad Malik says he went through a period of time as a kid, when he was not at all "cool."

His mixed ethnicity – his father is British Pakistani and his mother is English – made it tough to fit in at school. He was short for his age and, he admits, his haircuts were not always successful.

Flash forward to 2014: Guys don't come much cooler than Zayn.

Among One Direction members, Zayn's reputation is that of "The Vain One." He admits to fussing over his hair and clothes, often with the goal of making it look like he didn't fuss at all. A fan of body art, Zayn has added to his canvas at a pretty steady rate. Among his tattoos: a large microphone and cord on his right forearm, a lucky silver fern on the back of his neck, two Arabic inscriptions, a small yin-yang symbol on his left wrist, a stylized image of crossed fingers, a playing card tattoo on his chest and a heart on his hip.

Zayn has made headlines for his late-night partying, religion and sometimes inappropriate gestures. No aspect of his life, however, has been as well documented by the media as his romance with singer Perrie Edwards. The two started dating in fall 2011, got engaged in August 2013 and,

according to Zayn's mom, they plan to get married by late 2014.

"Perrie is a lovely girl and I get on really well with her," Trisha Malik told the BBC. "They're thinking of (getting married) the end of next year, although no date has yet been set yet."

And while the wedding date has not been set, Trisha is already thinking about her grandchildren. She hopes Zayn and Perrie buy a house close to hers.

"If they have children I wouldn't like to be so far away from them. I would really like to still be part of their lives," she said.

As for Perrie, she's obviously head-over-heels in love with the Bad Boy from Bradford. In a 2014 interview with MTV, she was asked about the best part about being engaged. Her answer, "(The best thing is) Just knowing that I am going to be with somebody that I love forever."

Ahhhh.

and charisma.

"It was clear very early that Liam was a natural talent," instructor Jodie Richards told the *Birmingham Mail* in October 2010.

Liam Payne

At the performing arts school Pink Productions, Liam James Payne is remembered as a shy boy who had natural ability

At the same time he was gaining confidence as a performer, the Wolverhampton, England, native was also participating in sports. He made the under-18 cross

when families stick together, I haven't said I agree with all that they've ever said," he said. He later returned to social media to remind the world that living his life under a microscope isn't easy: "I can't do anything without being judged. U try that and write about it."

No doubt, Liam hates the media scrutiny but he understands it's the price he must pay as one of the most recognizable celebrities in the world.

"The performing, the writing, the albums – all that is just more incredible than you could ever imagine," he told *Event* magazine in late 2013. "But none of us had any idea about the rest of it."

Harry Styles

Even if he wasn't a star, it's quite certain Harry Edward Styles' charisma, sense of humor and curly hair would make him a hit with the ladies. Being one-fifth of the world's most popular boy band ups his appeal quotient even higher.

Not only is Harry part of a phenomenally successful musical act, he is the most pop-

ular member of that act. Even fans devoted to Liam, Louis, Niall or Zayn can't argue with facts: Harry has 20.3 million Twitter followers, 2.2 million more than Niall, who comes in second among the five guys. He's

also won Teen Choice Awards for Male Hottie and Best Smile, and a Caprichio Award for International Male Hottie.

Harry, a native of Holmes Chapel,

Television talent shows have proven popular around the world. *The X Factor*, for instance, started in the United Kingdom and has aired in countries ranging from the United States and the Czech Republic to Albania and Australia.

One Direction didn't actually win *The X Factor* – they finished a respectable third – but they're among the most notable success stories to emerge from the show. As of early 2014, there have been a total of 114 winners of *The X Factor* worldwide. Here are a few others of note:

Leona Lewis

Leona Lewis was *The X Factor*'s 2006 champion. She has sold more than 20 million records worldwide; her first two albums reached No. 1 on the UK charts, with her third reaching No. 3.

Lewis, who so impressed music mogul Simon Cowell that he called her "the next Whitney Houston," has been nominated for seven Brit Awards and three Grammy Awards.

Olly Murs

Olly Murs didn't win *The X Factor*, but he came close. He made it to the 2009 finals, but lost the title to Joe McElderry.

Murs ended up singing a joint deal with Syco and Epic Records. In August 2013, he released his debut single, "Please DON'T Let Me Go," which debuted at No. 1 on the UK singles charts, becoming Murs' second top-ranked single after releasing "You Are Not Alone" with the other Season 6 *X Factor* finalists. The entertainer, known for his outspoken ways, has released three albums; the first reached No. 2 in the UK, while his latest two both hit the top spot.

Murs spent a chunk of 2012 in the United States, supporting One Direction on their first North American headline tour.

Sam Bailey

When Sam Bailey's *Power of Love* topped the UK's album charts in March 2014, she became the first X Factor winner since 2009 to have an album debut at No. 1.

Bailey, who won the tenth season of *The X Factor*, supported Beyonce on one of the dates of the UK leg of her 2014 world tour. The mother of two – she announced in March 2014 that she's pregnant with her third child – is scheduled to launch her first headline tour in January 2015.

Cher Lloyd

English rapper Cher Lloyd was signed by Simon Cowell to Syco Music after finishing fourth in the seventh season of *The X Factor*.

Her debut single "Swagger Jagger" entered at No. 1 on the UK Singles Chart and No. 2 in the Republic of Ireland when it was released in July 2011. Her debut album, *Sticks + Stones*, peaked at No. 4 in the United Kingdom. The musician has dipped her toes into the U.S. market, doing both radio station tours and performing on TV shows. In July 2012, her debut U.S. single, "Want U Back," shot to No. 7 on the iTunes chart.

In November 2013, during an interview with TV's Larry King, Lloyd confirmed that she left Syco Music after she and Cowell disagreed about her career path in music.

Her second studio album, *Sorry I'm Late*, is set for release in May 2014.

Cheshire, England, was charming the ladies long before he stepped up to his first microphone.

Born February 1, 1994, his mother, Ann Cox, told *The People* (London): "Ever since he was little, he has made people smile. I always thought he'd end up on the stage. He always loved attention and making people laugh. He's certainly not been shy about himself."

In recent years, Harry's gained a reputation as a real ladies' man. The list of those with whom he's reportedly been involved reads like a Who's Who Among the World's Most Stunning Women: singer and actress Caggie Dunlop, TV presenter Caroline Flack, radio DJ Lucy Horobin, models Emily Atack, Millie Brady, Kendall

Jenner, Emma Ostilly and Cara Delevingne, and singer Taylor Swift.

His cousin, Ben Selley, says Harry is simply a hopeless romantic.

"It's hard for Harry because he doesn't know whether a girl likes him for who he is or because he is famous," Selley told UK's *The Sun*. "It's something he struggles with because it's tricky. That's probably why he ends up dating people in the same industry as him."

When Harry's not busy quashing rumors about his love life, he's faced with gossip about leaked solo tracks and his plans to leave One Direction. But it's just that – gossip – says the group's rep. The music world is awaiting the next Justin Timberlake, who was a member of

N'SYNC before launching his thriving solo musical and acting career. Harry admires JT, but he's not ready to go it alone.

"We always hear rumors about us splitting — but we're not," Harry told *The Sun* in April 2014. "We've already started recording our fourth album."

Whew, there's a collective sigh of relief of 1D fans the world over.

Louis Tomlinson

Louis William Tomlinson is a Prankster – with a capital P.

He's been known to stick straws up Harry's nose while he's sleeping, he's tweeted fake messages to fans ("Can't believe I'm going to be a dad! Wow!") and he likes to switch up song lyrics – just to throw off his band mates.

"During a concert, I'll every now and then change a few words," he admitted to *E! News.* "I can't think of any off the top of my head, but something stupid and random."

That randomness keeps things light on stage and has earned Louis the adoration of fans who love to laugh at and with him.

Louis, born December 24, 1991, in Don-

caster, South Yorkshire, England, got his show business start as a very young child. Two of his stepsisters, Daisy and Phoebe, had roles as babies on a television drama called *Fat Friends*. When the girls worked, Louis would often tag along and serve as an extra. That early exposure to performing was enough to convince him that this was something he enjoyed.

He began attending an acting school in Barnsley and earned small roles in ITV's film *If I Had You* and BBC's *Waterloo Road*. He shined in school productions; his performance in *Grease* was memorable for two reasons:

1) The experience motivated him to audition for *The X Factor*.

2) He flashed his naked butt on stage during the show. That "exposure" earned him a weeklong suspension from school.

As goofy as Louis can be, he's obviously serious about his girlfriend, model Eleanor Calder. The two began dating in summer 2011 and Louis is the first to admit that making the relationship work while he's constantly on tour is difficult.

"I sometimes worry that she might want to go and find a boyfriend who's there every day," he told *Now* in January 2014. "Obviously it's not easy having a long-term relationship in this job, but it frustrates me when people say it's impossible. It's definitely doable, it's down to the people and whether they want to make it work enough."

Part of the "make it work" plan for these two: When Louis gets a day or two off, he's quick to fly back to London to visit his love and, in April 2014, he announced Eleanor will be joining the guys for parts of their *Where We Are* tour.

For a funny guy, it's clear Louis is serious about love.

CHAPTER TWO

TAKING THE WORLD BY STORM

Some musical acts blow into town, release a hit single or two, and blow away again. For One Direction, the breeze blowing them toward stardom has been more like an EF-5 tornado – and those 200-mile-per-hour winds show no signs of letting up.

Just how famous are the 1D guys? They're bigger than the Beatles, if you ask Harry Styles.

Harry told *Top of the Pops* magazine that watching the film of the Beatles arriving at JFK Airport in 1964 for their first-ever tour of the United States "really was like us ... Stepping off the plane, the girls, the madness, it was exactly the same as when we got there – just 50 years earlier."

A modest Mr. Styles added, "But none of us think we're in the same league as them music-wise. We'd be total fools if we did. Fame-wise it's probably even bigger, but we don't stand anywhere near them in terms of music."

Coldplay frontman Chris Martin thinks Harry's being too humble. He professed his love for 1D during an April 2014 interview with BBC Radio 1.

"I think One Direction are the biggest band in the world; their songs are great," he said. "I'm saying One Direction are brilliant and I'm not kidding. You know why? Because their songs are really good and I don't think that any of them are going to go solo. I think they appreciate their

chemistry, from watching their movie."

Martin is such a big fan that he and Coldplay covered "What Makes You Beautiful" during a 2012 concert in Florida. But Gwyneth Paltrow's Grammy-winning ex-husband is hardly the guys' only famous fan. Celebs have been singing One Direction's praises for years:

When the lads' single "Diana" was released in November 2013, singer Justin Bieber took to Twitter to applaud the track, writing, "That new 1D song Diana is well written. Well done boyzzzzzz."

Aly and AJ Michalka of 78Violet are big fans of the guys. The twin sisters, who were seen dancing the night away at a June 2013 1D concert in Las Vegas, proclaimed via Twitter: "Really love the melody of *Story of My Life* by @onedirection #digit."

English singer-songwriter Olly Murs, who also got his start thanks to *The X Factor*, has been an outspoken fan of 1D, often joking that he'd like to be the group's sixth member.

Katy Perry has been a fan of the group

from the beginning; she was actually a guest judge on *The X Factor*, back in 2010 when 1D was on the show. When the group made it to the top of the U.S. charts, Katy tweeted Niall: "Congratula-tions, you didn't let me down! xo"

An advance copy of One Direction's movie, *This Is Us*, was sent to the White House so that first daughters Malia and Sasha Obama could be the first to see it in America. A spokesman said: "They are

avid followers of One Direction and were thrilled to see their movie at the same time as the London premiere."

Joe Jonas, who first gained fame as a member of the boy band the Jonas Brothers, was an early fan of 1D. "I'm really liking One Direction's stuff," he told Scotland's *Daily Record*. "I met them at the (BBC Teen) awards and they were really nice, really cool, and I'm really happy for them. I think they're doing a great job and their stuff sounds great so I can definitely see myself checking out more of their music."

While fellow superstars may love One Direction, it's their millions of fans who have made them successful. The British pop group were the most popular global recording artists of 2013, outselling Eminem, Katy Perry and Justin Timberlake when it came to digital downloads, streaming and physical sales. Further proof of their enormity:

- ✪ Released in November 2013, 1D's album *Midnight Memories* hit No. 1 on the UK Albums Chart and was named the fastest and bestselling UK album of 2013 after selling 685,000 copies.
- ✪ One Direction's video for "The Best Song Ever" logged a record 10.9 million views during its first 24 hours of

BOY BAND BONANZA

One Direction has helped reignite music fans' appreciation for the boy band. These types of acts – relying perhaps a little heavier on choreography – ruled the music industry from the late 1980s to the early 2000s. Pop-punk and hip-hop took center stage for a while, but now the boy band phenomenon is back in full force.

Test your boy band knowledge by matching each song title to the boy band that made it a hit:

1. Big Time Rush	A. "I'll Be Loving You (Forever)"
2. Backstreet Boys	B. "Carry You"
3. After Romeo	C. "Music Sounds Better with U"
4. The Wanted	D. "She Looks So Perfect"
5. The Vamps	E. "Quit Playing Games (With My Heart)"
6. New Kids on the Block	F. "Chloe (You're the One I Want)"
7. Union J	G. "Love, Love"
8. Five Seconds of Summer	H. "Glad You Came"
9. Take That	I. "Free Fall"
10. Emblem3	J. "Wild Heart"

Answers: 1. C; 2. E; 3. I; 4. H; 5. J; 6. A; 7. B; 8. D; 9. G; 10. F

release according to Vevo, the record industry's official video platform for music videos.

- ✪ The band's 3D film, *This Is Us*, has earned more than $67.3 million worldwide, making it the fourth-highest-grossing concert movie of all time.
- ✪ In the two and a half years since releasing its debut album, One Direction has been nominated for 194 industry awards. The group has gone home with 139 of those trophies.
- ✪ In May 2013, One Direction broke the Guinness World Record for being the music group with the most

Twitter followers: 12,130,152. The One Direction fandom shows no signs of slowing down. The band currently has 18.8 million followers; the five guys' individual Twitter accounts have an additional 84 million follows – equal to the population of Egypt.

Music producer Simon Cowell, the mastermind behind TV talent shows *Pop Idol*, *The X Factor* and *Britain's Got Talent*, says he thought One Direction had potential, but he never imagined they'd become the superstars they have.

"We never predicted this," he told BBC Radio 2 in June 2013. "You could never predict this. All we knew is that we had

five talented guys ... They're very smart, these contestants. They knew exactly what kind of records they wanted to make. They're a really good example of having success but staying grounded."

Mark Hardy, a former Syco/Sony Music Entertainment marketing director, doesn't deny that the guys have talent, but he says the key to their popularity is that fans see them as relatable lads. Harry, Niall, Liam, Louis and Zayn weren't put on pedestals for fans to worship. Instead, the guys received extensive social media training and routinely send messages to fans via Twitter. They recorded songs about topics to which young girls could relate: new love, lost love, unrequited love. And they offered behind-the-scenes glimpses of themselves being actual guys – friends who hang out and have fun together.

"The essence of the strategy was not to position One Direction as demigods, but as 'my mate' who the girls could have access to 24/7," Hardy told *Retail Week* in September 2013. Hardy says talent plus

interaction and collaboration, plus "making the boys feel really accessible," has played a played a role in their success.

Accessible? Yes.

Talented? Yes.

Handsome? Yes.

But is it possible those attributes have combined to make One Direction bigger than the Beatles, a band that's widely

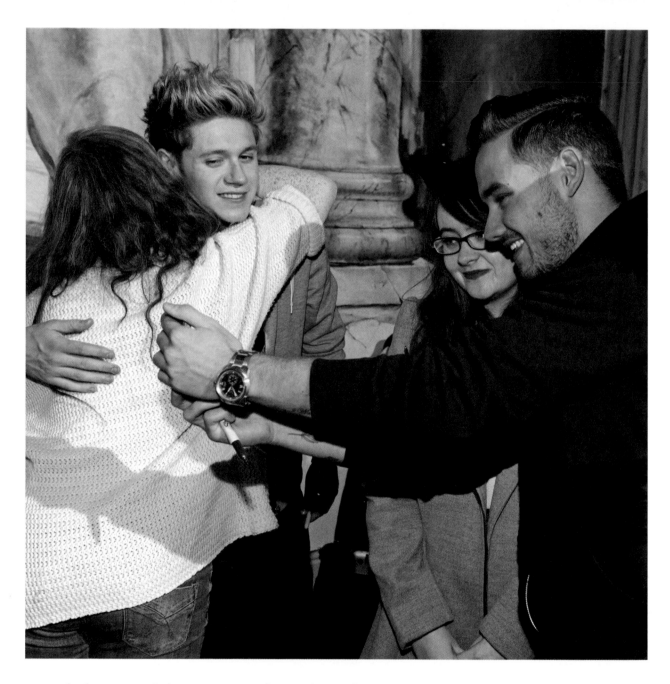

regarded as one of the most popular and influential acts in the history of rock music? Perhaps.

Even Beatles member Paul McCartney can't deny 1D's ever-increasing popularity.

In October 2013, McCartney told UK-based *Sky News:* "I like One Direction. They're young, beautiful boys and that's the big attraction ... they can sing, they make good records, so I think that's what I would see in common (with the Beatles). Girls love them."

Love, love, love them. Yes, Sir Paul, girls really do.

CHAPTER THREE
MAKING MEMORIES

One Direction's latest album, *Midnight Memories*, was released in late November 2013 and quickly became the fastest-selling album in Amazon UK's 15-year history, breaking the record set by 1D's 2012 release, *Take Me Home*. As impressive as that sales statistic is, there's more:

- The CD shot to No. 1 in 31 countries including the United Kingdom, United States, Canada, Australia, Spain, Ireland, Turkey, Croatia, Japan, India, Taiwan and Thailand.
- According to Sony Music, *Midnight Memories* was No. 1 on iTunes charts in 97 countries.
- Despite its end-of-the-year-release, *Midnight Memories* edged out Emeli Sandé's *Our Version of Events* to become 2013's biggest-selling album in the United Kingdom.
- According to Nielsen SoundScan, One

Direction's third studio release was the eighth-biggest-selling CD in the United States in 2013, with 714,000 copies sold in just five weeks.

One Direction started work on *Midnight Memories* while on the road with their *Take Me Home* Tour. Band members immediately began talking about wanting the new album to be more "mature" than their previous releases; more rock and less pop sounding. The end product pays homage to 1980s rock, a genre that Bon Jovi and Aerosmith-loving Liam Payne adores.

American songwriter and producer Julian Bunetta, who worked with the guys on many of the songs on *Midnight Memories,* told MTV News that the name of the album and message behind its title track came quite naturally, from the circumstances under which it was recorded.

"Midnight memories are where most of the memories of this record were made. (It) was between midnight and 5 in the

morning," he said. "We have so many memories of just being in the studio or being after a show or being in the back of the bus or going to one of the guy's places and hanging and writing. Or, (it's also) just

when you're young and that's when you kind of have all your experiences."

Bunetta said the album was constructed with the knowledge that One Direction was launching a stadium tour, so songs needed to work whether they were being

played on a stage in front of tens of thousands of people or in the privacy of a fan's bedroom.

In an effort to personalize the project, the band's five members contributed lyrics to 12 of the 14 songs on the standard edition (plus another three on the deluxe 18-track). When a fan took to Twitter to share her excitement at hearing the folk-rock track "Happily," she got a response from Savan Kotecha, who worked extensively with One Direction on their first two albums. "I'm excited for everyone to hear it. @*Harry_Styles* is one hell of a writer!" the award-winning songwriter and producer tweeted.

Liam said that, while he and the rest of the guys relished the opportunity to play a bigger role in songwriting this time around, fans shouldn't expect a total transformation in the band's sound or look.

MIDNIGHT MEMORIES: TRACKS AT A GLANCE

1. "Best Song Ever" – The lead single from Midnight Memories, this song's music video was filmed in Miami over two days. The tune's tight group harmonies make it infectious.

2. "Story of My Life" – All five guys had a hand in writing this song. Its lyrics tell the story of a rocky relationship that ultimately leads to heartbreak.

3. "Diana" – Who's Diana? Louis told Perez TV: "We were actually working with a few different names for the chorus, and the top name originally was 'Joanna,' which is actually quite close to my mum's name and it felt a little weird, so we changed it to Diana."

4. "Midnight Memories" – Liam and Louis are listed among this song's writers; it was the third single from the album. You'll come for the guitar licks and stay for the rocking chorus.

5. "You and I" – This song, reportedly Zayn's favorite on the album, is perfect for slow dancing with your sweetie.

6. "Don't Forget Where You Belong" – The members of English pop rock band McFly wrote this rock ballad with Niall.

7. "Strong" – Louis helped pen this upbeat, but earnest, love song.

8. "Happily" – Harry wrote this song alongside Savan Kotecha, Carl Falk and Kristian Lundin. Listen up for the banjo and foot stomps.

9. "Right Now" – OneRepublic hit-maker Ryan Tedder helped the guys write this ode to life on the road.

10. "Little Black Dress" – This track is a little more raucous than the other songs on the album. It's a real hands-in-the-air-dance-to-every-beat kind of tune.

11. "Through the Dark" – Liam and Louis helped write this folksy song that's filled with inspiration and encouragement.

12. "Something Great" – Snow Patrol's Gary Lightbody joined forces with 1D to create this guitar-driven cut.

13. "Little White Lies" – This energetic song brings with it a big dose of 1980s arena-rock.

14. "Better Than Words" – If you like ballads, you'll love this one; it's where the guys shine brightest.

BONUS TRACKS
"Why Don't We Go There"
"Does He Know?"
"Alive"
"Half a Heart"

"(We) had the chance to work with a lot of great writers and stuff, but we just made it a bit more edgier," he told MTV during a mid-2013 interview about the band's new release. "Just subtle changes here and there, so it kind of grows as we grow."

Those subtle changes struck a chord with fans.

The album's lead single, "Best Song Ever," was released on July 22, 2013. The song's music video beat the Vevo record for most viewers within 24 hours on YouTube. Its 12.3 million views beat the previous record set by Miley Cyrus of 10.7 million views in 24 hours for "We Can't Stop."

"Story of My Life," a guitar-driven tune,

was released October 28, 2013, as the second single from *Midnight Memories*. The song peaked at No. 1 in at least eight countries, including the United States, Ireland and Spain. The single's music video starts in a dark room with the band developing photos and features some of the guys' family members: Zayn Malik's sister, Harry Styles' mother, Liam's parents and sisters, Niall Horan's brother and Louis Tomlinson's grandparents. The heart-warming video has earned widespread praise. Even often-critical music mogul Simon Cowell took to Twitter to proclaim: "I think the Story Of My Life is the best One D video yet. And I love the record."

"Midnight Memories" was released as the third single on November 20, 2013, just five days before the release of the album.

Liam took to YouTube to announce the single. "Our next single is going to be 'Midnight Memories,' which is one of the songs I wrote with Louis. This is the first song we wrote on the album and it paved the way for this whole album's sound and the way it all changes," he said. "It's a big, big tune, it's all about the midnight memories, everyone's got them, so I hope you enjoy it." The song debuted at No.

3 on the Irish Singles Chart and broke into the Top 10 in at least nine additional countries.

Bunneta, who also worked with the 1D guys on their second album, said teaming up with the guys on their newest project was fun, busy and exhausting.

"There were deadlines," he told MTV. "There were boundaries because you can't

just spend all night with them, at least, in the studio. They have a certain amount of time; they have an insanely busy schedule. ... Because we had deadlines, we would have to make decisions on the fly that were either gonna be the right call and be brilliant or wouldn't work out."

"And so it gave us a pressure situation and I think people who are great at whatever, they do thrive with that. I like a bit of chaos," he said, likening the whole experience to being at a grown-up sleepover. "It was wild: new cities, new experiences, new things. It was so fun."

CHAPTER FOUR
TOURING THE WORLD

The One Direction crew will be collecting plenty of stamps in their passports in 2014. The guys' first stadium tour, "Where We Are," has them performing 69 dates on three continents: South America, Europe and North America.

"Where We Are", 1D's third headlining concert tour, was announced by the guys during a May 16, 2013, press conference at London's Wembley Stadium. The tour officially kicked off April 25, 2014, at El Campín Stadium in Bogotá, Colombia, and is in support of the band's third studio album, *Midnight Memories*.

The One Direction crew are no strangers to big venues. They ended 2012 selling out Madison Square Garden in less than 10 minutes and, in 2013, they took their "Take Me Home" tour to Europe, America, Canada, Mexico, Australia, New Zealand and Japan – while winning a BRIT Award,

two American Music Awards, three Billboard Music Awards, six Teen Choice Awards and an MTV Video Music Award along the way.

The group's 2014 tour includes 31 dates in 21 North American cities; along the way, they will perform in 14 of the biggest stadiums in the NFL.

Because their tickets were snatched up nearly as soon as their shows were announced, the resale or secondary market has become the go-to place for Directioners who must see their boys. According to the website TiqIQ, the average price for One Direction tickets across their North American dates is $239.72 on the secondary market. Tickets for some of the shows are substantially more expensive; the average price secondary ticket for 1D's September 2014 show at El Paso's Sun Bowl Stadium, for example, is $530. And, it should come as no surprise that, according to ticket marketplace Viagogo, 1D tickets were the most searched-for tickets throughout all of 2013.

With all that cash being shelled out for tickets, the pressure is on to make sure fans are getting what they pay for. Early indications are that the show does not disappoint.

While in South America, on the tour's first stops, the guys opened their shows with the title track of their current album, "Midnight Memories," and ended with their massive hit "Best Song Ever." A majority of their recent album tracks are also

on the set list, as well as hit singles including "One Thing," "What Makes You Beautiful," "Kiss You," "Live While We're Young" and "Little Things."

In addition to their music, the guys are also entertaining fans by answering Instagram video questions during their shows. One Direction members answered Twitter questions during their 2013 "Take Me Home" tour, which led to some amusing moments. The show is less choreographed than what you'd expect to see from artists such as Justin Bieber or Selena Gomez, but the guys' sliding around and riding piggyback onstage is more than enough entertainment to elicit fans' repeated and high-pitched squeals of approval.

For all the fun that goes along with a world tour, it takes a lot of hard work and the process can be, at times, overwhelming.

In 2013, for example, One Direction's

bosses enrolled the guys in Zumba and spin classes to get them in shape for their "Take Me Home" tour. No word on whether a fitness regimen was part of this year's tour prep, but the guys have acknowledged they've been strongly encouraged to eat right and get plenty of sleep.

"It's important for us that we kind of make each tour bigger and better than the one before," Harry told Capital FM in April 2014. "We want everyone to come and enjoy the show. (Even) if they're a dad, if they're not necessarily a fan, we want them to still feel like they've seen a show and go away and say, 'Actually they're quite good.' It's important that we make sure the show and the music and everything stays very exciting."

OPENING ACT:
5 SECONDS OF SUMMER

The Australian pop-punk group 5 Seconds of Summer first gained celebrity status in 2013, after opening for One Direction on the bulk of its arena tour. And now they're back: 5SOS will rejoin 1D again in 2014, as the opening act for stadium stops across Europe and North America.

The teenage band from Western Sydney, comprised of Michael Clifford, Calum Hood, Luke Hemmings and Ashton Irwin, joins 1D's "Where We Are" tour starting May 23, 2014, in Ireland.

5 Seconds of Summer played a short spring 2014 tour in their homeland and were among performers confirmed for the Billboard Music Awards in Las Vegas. Their debut four-track EP, *She Looks So Perfect*, opened at No. 2 on the Billboard 200 when it was released in April 2014.

The Capitol Records recording artists will release their debut full-length album on July 22, 2014, a date selected for maximum exposure from the "Where We Are" tour.

Yes, these guys are still teenagers.

Yes, they're talented and handsome.

Yes, Louis Tomlinson gave them a giant boost when he took to Twitter to declare his love for them back in November 2012.

But make no mistake: 5SOS is not just simply a slightly younger version of One Direction. For starters, 5SOS have carefully underlined the fact that they all play instruments. And all you have to do is take a quick listen to hear that their sound is considerably edgier and darker than One Direction's.

Similar but not the same. That's probably what makes these bands such great tourmates.

Even with fans shrieking their adoration, the guys say it's difficult to be away from family, friends and girlfriends for months on end. Liam Payne, for one, had a very rough go of it when the guys embarked on their "Where We Are" tour in April 2014. He posted some cryptic but sorrowful messages on his Twitter:

"Can't be without you"

"Worse (sic) thing I ever did was let you go."

"Now all I got left is the thought of you."

Liam had been dating Sophia Smith, but the two reportedly called it quits just prior to this world tour. Liam is said to be heartbroken, but the couple agreed that the distance would make their relationship too difficult to maintain.

"He's devastated that it's over but it was for the best. They were spending too much time apart and it's only going to get worse this year – the band going on a super long tour, her getting busier with university ... Too much long distance," a source close to the band told *US Weekly*.

"It was draining for the both of them and led to a lot of arguments. Liam was the one who chose to end it. There was no way to maintain the relationship. He had to do it as they would never see each other and he didn't think it was fair to her."

The insider said Liam's bandmates were concerned about him and were working to help him through the rough patch.

"The boys know the tour is going to be draining for them all, but they're committed to giving Liam the extra support he needs," the source said.

For his part, Liam told *The* (London) *Sun*

he's excited to be back on tour.

"Coming back together is like the first day of school. We don't want to go into the lessons because the social is too much fun," he said following one of 1D's South American shows. "Being on the road is quite lonely, especially being sat in a hotel room. I hate being by myself. A lot of us aren't really used to being on our own."

To fight the lonelies, all the boys are planning to meet up with family and friends while on tour. Zayn Malik and Louis Tomlinson will be joined by their gal pals, Perrie Edwards and Eleanor Calder,

respectively. Liam has friends flying in so he can "spend time with the lads." And Niall Horan's father will connect with the gang in Italy to both see his son perform and do some sightseeing.

And, of course, the 1D chaps know they're really never alone when tens of thousands of fans are in the audience, singing along at every show.

"One Direction fans are just so solid," Niall told *Teen Vogue*. "Our fans have put us where we are and it's amazing."

You can say that again ... amazing.

ONE DIRECTION WORLD TOUR DATES

April 25, 2014	Estadio El Campin, Bogota, Colombia
April 27, 2014	Estadio Nacional, Lima, Peru
April 30, 2014	Estadio Nacional, Santiago, Chile
May 1, 2014	Estadio Nacional, Santiago, Chile
May 3, 2014	Velez Sarsfield, Buenos Aires, Argentina
May 4, 2014	Velez Sarsfield, Buenos Aires, Argentina
May 6, 2014	Estadio Centenario, Montevideo, Uruguay
May 8, 2014	Parque dos Atletas, Rio De Janeiro, Brazil
May 10, 2014	Estádio do Morumbi, Sao Paulo, Brazil
May 11, 2014	Estádio do Morumbi, Sao Paulo, Brazil
May 23, 2014	Croke Park, Dublin, Ireland
May 24, 2014	Croke Park, Dublin, Ireland
May 24, 2014	Glasgow Green/Radio 1's Big Weekend, Glasgow, Scotland
May 25, 2014	Croke Park, Dublin, Ireland
May 28, 2014	Stadium Of Light, Sunderland, England
May 30, 2014	Etihad Stadium, Manchester, England
May 31, 2014	Etihad Stadium, Manchester, England
June 1, 2014	Etihad Stadium, Manchester, England
June 3, 2014	Murrayfield Stadium, Edinburgh, Scotland
June 6, 2014	Wembley Stadium, London, England
June 7, 2014	Wembley Stadium, London, England
June 8, 2014	Wembley Stadium, London, England
June 13, 2014	Friends Arena, Stockholm, Sweden
June 14, 2014	Friends Arena, Stockholm, Sweden
June 16, 2014	National Stadium Parken, Copenhagen, Denmark
June 17, 2014	National Stadium Parken, Copenhagen, Denmark
June 20, 2014	Stade de France, Paris, France
June 21, 2014	Stade de France, Paris, France
June 24, 2014	Amsterdam Arena, Amsterdam, The Netherlands
June 25, 2014	Amsterdam Arena, Amsterdam, The Netherlands
June 28, 2014	Stadio San Siro, Milan, Italy
June 29, 2014	Stadio San Siro, Milan, Italy

July 2, 2014	Esprit Arena, Dusseldorf, Germany
July 4, 2014	Stade de Suisse, Berne, Switzerland
July 6, 2014	Stadio Olimpico, Turin, Italy
July 8, 2014	Estadi Olimpic, Barcelona, Spain
July 10, 2014	Vincente Calderon, Madrid, Spain
July 11, 2014	Vincente Calderon, Madrid, Spain
July 13, 2014	Dragao Stadium, Porto, Portugal
August 1, 2014	Canada Rogers Centre, Toronto, Ontario
August 2, 2014	Canada Rogers Centre, Toronto, Ontario
August 4, 2014	MetLife Stadium, East Rutherford, New Jersey
August 5, 2014	MetLife Stadium, East Rutherford, New Jersey
August 7, 2014	Gillette Stadium, Foxboro, Massachusetts
August 8, 2014	Gillette Stadium, Foxboro, Massachusetts
August 11, 2014	Nationals Park, Washington DC
August 13, 2014	Lincoln Financial Field, Philadelphia, Pennsylvania
August 14, 2014	Lincoln Financial Field, Philadelphia, Pennsylvania
August 16, 2014	Ford Field, Detroit, Michigan
August 17, 2014	Ford Field, Detroit, Michigan
August 19, 2014	LP Field, Nashville, Tennessee
August 22, 2014	Reliant Stadium, Houston, Texas
August 24, 2014	AT&T Stadium, Dallas, Texas
August 27, 2014	Edward Jones Dome, St.Louis, Missouri
August 29, 2014	Soldier Field, Chicago, Illinois
August 30, 2014	Soldier Field, Chicago, Illinois
September 11, 2014	Rose Bowl, Pasadena, California
September 12, 2014	Rose Bowl, Pasadena, California
September 13, 2014	Rose Bowl, Pasadena, California
September 16, 2014	Phoenix Stadium, Phoenix, Arizona
September 19, 2014	Sun Bowl Stadium, El Paso, Texas
September 21, 2014	Alamodome, San Antonio, Texas
September 23, 2014	BOK Center, Tulsa, Oklahoma
September 25, 2014	Mercedes-Benz Superdome, New Orleans, Louisiana
September 27, 2014	PNC Music Pavilion, Charlotte, North Carolina
September 28, 2014	PNC Music Pavilion, Charlotte, North Carolina
October 1, 2014	Georgia Dome, Atlanta, Georgia
October 3, 2014	Raymond James Stadium, Tampa, Florida
October 5, 2014	Sun Life Stadium, Miami, Florida

CHAPTER FIVE
TALENTED & RICH

Thanks to the sale of concert tickets, albums, DVDs and tons of merchandise, One Direction is set to earn a massive $1 billion dollars by the end of 2014 – that's not million, but BILLION. That means Niall Horan, Liam Payne, Louis Tomlinson, Harry Styles and Zayn Malik are not only talented and handsome, they're also extraordinarily wealthy.

The math geniuses at *Business Insider* magazine didn't actually get a look at the guys' bank statements, but some simple addition and multiplication has led them to proclaim that by the end of 2014, One Direction, the hottest musical act on the planet, will likely be the first billion dollar boy band.

Concert ticket sales will account for the largest chunk of the guys' paychecks, the magazine projected in its August 2013 issue. Based on a conservative average ticket price of $75, 1D's "Where We Are"

world tour should bring in more than $270 million. When added to the estimated $187.5 million in gross revenue from its 2013 "Take Me Home" tour, it's thought the band's total earnings from the concerts will be somewhere around $457.5 million.

While fans were busy laughing at the guys' crazy antics – both on and off stage – in their *This Is Us* movie, the guys and their management were laughing all the way to the bank. It's estimated One Direction will gross around $125 million for ticket and DVD sales of its 3D movie. One Direction should also realize $300 million for record sales and $15 million for sales of *Up All Night: The Live Tour DVD*.

But don't put those calculators away just yet. The One Direction lads are merchandising marvels. Their images are printed

tions released a line of One Direction dolls in late 2011. The dolls, which measure 12 to 13 inches tall, retail for upwards of $20 each. And, don't forget the guys' successful perfume One Moment, and their

or screened or embossed on everything you can imagine: bedding, beach towels, pillows, posters, key chains, jewelry, lunch boxes, backpacks, clocks, ear buds, stickers, door hangers, T-shirts, hoodies, phone cases and more. Toymaker Vivid Imagina-

soon-to-be-released second scent, That Moment. The magazine estimates sales of all these "extras" at just under $70 million.

In May 2014, the UK *Sunday Times* declared One Direction the richest boy band in British history. *The Daily Mail* reported

the group's total net worth at $117.7 million. That's a whole lot of cash – especially when you consider this band didn't even exist until late 2010.

"There hasn't been another boy band who have made so much money so quickly," said the rich list's editor Ian Coxon. "Whether they will carry on at the same rate is anybody's guess."

The guys are working hard for their money, so it's no surprise that they're finding joy in spending some of it on luxury cars and high-end homes, both in the United States and the United Kingdom. Harry has a reputation – perhaps deserved – as the biggest spender among the five. According to *The* (London) *Daily Mail*, Harry has an Audi R8 coupe worth $168,000, a 1970s Ford Capri and a Range Rover Sport worth up to $135,000; he also owns a $4.4 million mansion in Los Angeles, a $5 million home in north London and a $967,000

PERFUME LAUNCH, TAKE TWO

One Direction's debut fragrance, One Moment, has been a sweet-smelling success. Launched in June 2013 in London, the line includes eau de parfum, a shower gel, a body lotion and a rollerball.

Now, the guys – aided by professional perfumists – are gearing up to unveil fragrance No. 2: a special edition perfume called That Moment. The new cologne project was announced by the band in February 2014.

According to Harry Styles, the second fragrance was inspired by fans.

"Your reaction to Our Moment has been absolutely amazing," he said in a video announcement. "We're so, so pleased that you guys like it so much, and people have already been asking what is next for Our Moment, so we've come up with a new version of Our Moment."

Their scent sequel, according to Harry, comes "with some of the original notes but with some new stuff, so it's taking things like pink grapefruit and jasmine and mixing them with new scents like apple and violet in a swanky new bottle."

According to the online beauty retailer feelunique, Our Moment was the best-selling famous fragrance of Christmas 2013. One Direction's fragrance sold at least five times more than any other celebrity fragrance for the holidays.

Siobhan McDermott, feelunique general manager, told the (London) *Mirror*: "This just proves that women will quite literally do anything to have Harry Styles' scent on their skin."

Who are the runners up in the celebrity fragrance arena? Lady Gaga is a strong second place with her 18th Century-inspired Fame perfume. Pop princess Britney Spears comes in third with her fragrance Fantasy and Nicki Minaj's scent, Pink Friday, comes in fourth.

Justin Bieber's fragrance, The Key, finished the year at No. 5, and Taylor Swift's Wonderstruck – which was the biggest celebrity seller of 2012, finished 2013 in sixth place.

If you think celebrity fragrances are a new phenomenon, think again. International film star Sophia Loren debuted Sophia in 1981. Singer and actress Cher launched a musky Uninhibited in 1987. And actress Elizabeth Taylor's White Diamonds, which was launched back in 1991, continues to be a hit; over the years the perfume has made more than $1 billion, and in 2013 alone, it earned a whopping $10 million.

flat in east London.

Greg Horan told the *Irish Sun* in August 2013 that he didn't expect mega-wealth to change his younger brother. "I think he will cope well whatever happens. Niall doesn't spend that much money or talk about money; it's not a big thing in his life. Obviously it's amazing if the band go on to make a billion in a year and I for one hope they do — but it will not change Niall, I know that much," he said. Considering Niall's indifference toward cash, he's managed to make some major investments. One Direction's only Irish member reportedly owns homes in London and Los Angeles, worth $3.7 million and $2.5 million, respectively.

The other boys also have made some

notable purchases. Zayn bought himself a $3.7 million mansion in north London and a $471,000 home for his mother. Louis has a $151,000 Range Rover and a $4.2 million home in north London. And Liam, who appears to be the most frugal of the lot, has a $3.4 million flat in London's Canary Wharf financial district.

As much as they love spending their cash, the One Direction fellows continue to make it a priority to give back through charitable organizations. According to the social change organization DoSomething.org, the 1D guys were 2013's most charitable celebrities worldwide, topped only by country-pop singer Taylor Swift.

In recognizing the band's philanthropic efforts, the sixth annual Top 20 Celebs Gone Good list noted that One Direction kicked off 2013 by recording a cover of Blondie's classic hit "One Way or Another" with all proceeds helping those affected by famine in Africa. The fivesome also flew to Ghana with U.K. charity Comic Relief's Red Nose Day to visit schools and hos-

pitals, where they met with children who were dying from preventable diseases.

"It was incredibly eye-opening for us all," Harry told *Teen Vogue*.

Niall called the trip life-changing and told entertainmentwise.com, "It was unbelievable, we had an amazing time. Even before we'd left on the plane to come back to London, we asked them could we go back. I don't think people believe how poor these people are until they see it. It was tough to see."

Their charitable contributions are as diverse as the guys are. Harry and Liam have

raised more than $800,000 through the fundraising platform Prizeo for Trekstock, a London-based nonprofit that supports cancer research. The guys have also raised money for organizations including the Alzheimer's Association, BBC Children in Need, Teenage Cancer Trust, Greenpeace and Mines Advisory Group. In May 2014, the Niall Horan Charity Football Challenge was set to raise money for three charities: the Foxes Foundation, Irish

Autism Action and another autism charity, the UK Heart and Minds Challenge.

Naomi Hirabayashi, chief marketing officer of DoSomething.org, hailed One Direction's charitable giving in a news release, saying: "This rising generation is using their money and star power for good."

One Direction: talented, rich and using their star power to make the world a better place.

CHAPTER SIX

DIRECTIONERS ROCK

"Two hours of high-pitched squeals. That's what you get when you go to a One Direction show," declared Radio.com associate music producer Shannon Carlin after attending a 1D show at the IZOD Center in East Rutherford, New Jersey.

One Directioners, as 1D Fans are known, are an enthusiastic group known for both their loyalty and their loudness.

"It's Biebermania multiplied by five," wrote (London) *Daily Mail* reporter Leah McDonald in an attempt to explain how – and why – One Direction Infection has become a worldwide epidemic.

Even their first televised American concert in March 2012 attracted more than 10,000 screaming fans. A while later, in Nashville, dozens of girls chased the band's car down Music Row. And, when word got out that the guys would be stopping by Washington, D.C., radio station

99.5 FM, fans showed up by the thousands – some of them a full eight days before their two-song concert.

These days, the band's super fans have a reputation as one of the most dedicated fan groups of the Internet age. More than 103.5 million Directioners follow their favorite musicians on Twitter, while 5.2 million follow them on Instagram; 1D's official Facebook pages has more than 30.2 million "likes" and another 13.2 million fans subscribe to the band's Vevo channel.

Musician Olly Murs, who has his own legion of faithful fans, has opened shows for two of One Direction's tours. He says nothing prepared him for passion Directioners have for their guys.

"I have never seen anything like it," Murs told *Kent Online.* "Girls were running after the buses. It was quite dangerous at times, they are insane but their response was amazing … It was very loud."

The One Direction guys have millions of fans around the world and sometimes, in the heat of the moment, they become

overwhelmed. Overwhelmed fans, it seems, are prone to fainting.

During an August 2013 interview with Yahoo, Liam Payne confessed that it is "mad" when it happens to girls in their audiences.

"I remember the first few gigs we ever did," he said. "The first few gigs we did were like in some night club and it was really like round and these girls were fainting and getting pulled out of the audience.

And it was just like, it's just the strangest thing ever. It's just mad."

And, the guys say that no matter how long they do this, they may never get used to fans' reactions.

"It's never not got to feel weird, someone like screaming at you," Harry Styles told Yahoo.

Occasionally the fanaticism of One Direction fans goes a little overboard. When the band performed in Peru in April 2014, the crowd pushed toward the stage and crushed more than 40 concertgoers who were treated for symptoms of asphyxia and other injuries. Over the past few years, band members' girlfriends have received death threats from overzealous fans. Others have taken to social media to offer to chop off limbs or kill kittens in an effort to capture the attention of the 1D guys.

Documentary filmmaker Daisy Asquith

SIMON SAYS

Simon Cowell is the brash and snarky music mogul who is the mastermind behind TV talent shows *Pop Idol, The X Factor* and *Britain's Got Talent.* He mentored One Direction during the 2010 season of *The X Factor* and eventually signed the boys to his music label.

Simon, who has never been one to bite his tongue, has had many things to say to and about One Direction over the past few years. A few of his more notable comments include:

To *Rolling Stone* in April 2012: "I met them as solo artists to begin with. Each of them individually had very good auditions. We had high hopes for two or three of them in particular, and then it all kind of fell apart at one of the latter stages. Interestingly, when they left, I had a bad feeling that maybe we shouldn't have lost them and maybe there was something else we should do with them. And this is when the idea came about that we should see if they could work as a group. We invited these five guys back. They were the only five we cared about. The minute they stood there for the first time together – it was a weird feeling. They just looked like a group at that point.

"(I knew they were going to be huge) after about a millionth of a second ... The second they left I jumped out of my chair and said, 'These guys are incredible!' They just had it. They had this confidence. They were fun. They worked out the arrangements themselves. They were like a gang of friends, and kind of fearless as well."

To MTV News in September 2012: "The world right now is theirs."

To *The* (London) *Sun* in March 2013: "I'd be as wild as them at their age."

To BBC Radio in June 2013: "We never predicted this. You could never predict this. All we knew is that we had five talented guys. They're interesting, both One Direction and Little Mix. They're very smart, these contestants. They knew exactly what kind of records they wanted to make. They're a really good example of having success but staying grounded."

On *Chelsea Lately* in July 2013: "I liked them all individually, but for whatever reason, nerves or whatever, they didn't make it through to the next round. But I liked these boys and I thought you know what, let's give them another shot."

On *The Tonight Show* with Jay Leno in September 2013: "I couldn't predict what would happen, but it was fantastic."

To *Billboard* magazine in November 2013: "Eventually they probably will split up and maybe want to have their own careers."

Via Twitter in January 2014: "So one direction were the biggest selling artists in 2013. I know how much they put into this record from start to finish. Very proud."

Via Twitter following the February 2014 Brit Awards: "Congratulations One D! Global success of the year. So happy for you."

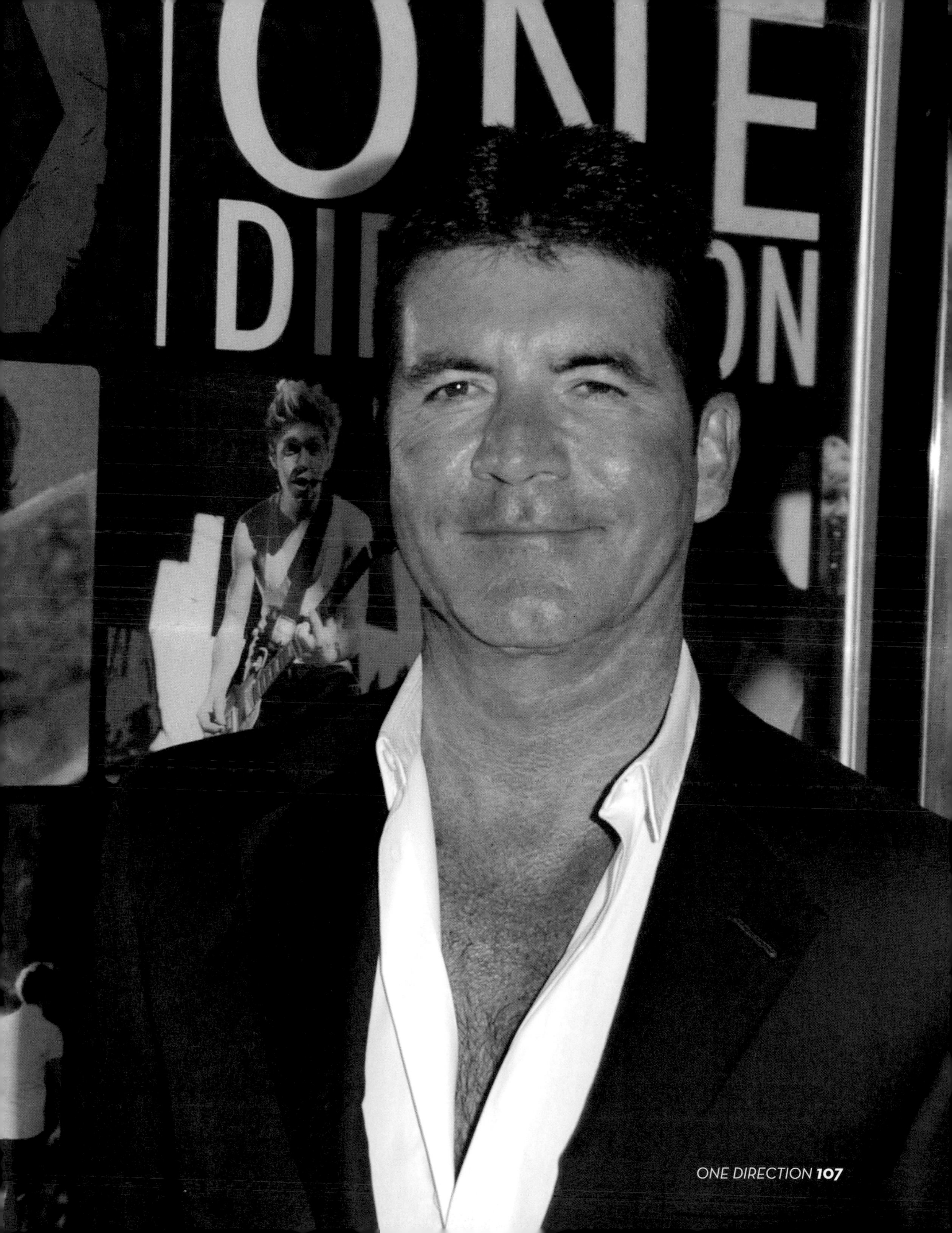
ONE
DI
ON

set out to find out why the band has become so idolized by so many people so quickly. While making her film, *Crazy About One Direction*, Asquith joined the guys' legion of fans for a three-month period.

"It gave me an idea why girls would choose to wait for 21 hours in the freezing rain outside a venue, only to meet their idols for two minutes or maybe not at all," she told *Radio Times* in August 2013. The British filmmaker marveled at the way the fans reach out to the band members via Twitter. She said on those rare occasions when the guys actually respond, "it's earth-shatteringly exciting."

"I think that's what makes it so addictive," she said. "They have this proximity

to the band that teenage fans have never had before. The 'hunt,' as they call it, is also exciting."

Asquith stops short of decoding the psychology of teenage girls but notes: "I was working out why they need to be in this gang, and what they get out of it. I think it is about not being with the boys so much as being with each other."

The band does have its doubters, often in the form of teenage boys who are jealous that girls seem more interested in Harry and the gang than they do about their own classmates. And, admittedly, the guys have, from time to time, had to call for extra security to handle rowdy followers or change hotel rooms when raucous admirers blocked the entrances. Still, One Direction loves its fervent fan base.

"There's nothing not to like," Niall Horan told *Billboard* magazine, "our fans are the best fans in the world."

That gratitude is sincere because, as well as they sing and as cool as they look, Harry, Niall, Liam, Louis and Zayn know it's

the fans who've gotten them where they are today.

"There's just no way to kind of comprehend it," Harry told the (Scottish) *Daily Record* in May 2014. "You never imagine

that anything gets to this level and we're just so happy and so, so grateful for everything. The fans have made it all happen and it's insane."

As far as One Direction has come since its reality TV show debut, it's important to remember that these guys are young and could – potentially – be performing together for years to come. Heck, the Roll-

ing Stones were formed in London back in 1962 and – despite a handful of personnel changes over the years – the band still tours today. In fact, the Stones, with septuagenarian Mick Jagger at the helm, had the sixth highest grossing concert tour of 2013.

Is it likely One Direction will still be together and touring five decades from now? No one knows for sure what will happen, but the guys say they're not ready to go their separate ways yet – not for a while at least.

"We by no means think we've done it all and think we haven't got anything left to do," Harry told the *Daily Record*. "I think we've got so much that we still want to do and a lot of things we still want to achieve. And get better and better as performers and as singers."